D1067820

THE COFFEE HOUSES & PALACES OF VIENNA

THE COFFEE HOUSES & PALACES OF VIENNA

Commentary
SANDY LESBERG

PEEBLES PRESS
New York   London

FIRST PUBLISHED 1976 BY
PEEBLES PRESS INTERNATIONAL
12 Thayer St., London W1M 5LD
10 Columbus Circle, New York, N.Y. 10019

Designed by Nicolai Canetti

© Peebles Press International (Europe) Ltd
ISBN 0–672–52227–6
Library of Congress Catalog No. 75–36326

The publishers wish to acknowledge with great gratitude the splendid assistance
and co-operation they have received in the preparation of this book
Austrian National Tourist Office and the Vienna City Tourist Board.

Distributed by
The Bobbs-Merrill Co. Inc.
4300 West 62nd St., Indianapolis, Indiana 46268, U.S.A.
in the United States and Canada

WHS Distributors
Euston St., Freemen's Common, Leicester, England
in the U.K., Ireland, Australia, New Zealand and South Africa

Meulenhoff-Bruna B.V.
Beulingstraat 2, Amsterdam, Netherlands
in the Netherlands

Printed and bound in the U.K. by
Redwood Burn Limited, Trowbridge and Esher

Vienna is one of the truly great romantic capitals of Europe. Politically, culturally and scientifically its credentials are impeccable and its background fascinating. Here was the seat of the far flung Hapsburg Empire, ruled by Empress Maria Theresa, with many of its great palaces still maintained in what some might crassly describe as "move-in condition". Schönbrunn Palace on the outskirts of the city was the summer house where now Sunday visitors from all over the world wander the stately rooms and vast grounds, and wonder about how life really was back in those halcyon emperical days. The power and the influence has long been drained but the feeling of majesty remains, engendered by the easy availability of these monuments of a bygone era, to all who would walk through the hallowed halls. Even now the buildings remain the same while the politics has changed immeasurably, the royalty has become history and Austria has now become an indispensable neutral between the diplomatic interests of the East and the West.

This was not always so. Not so long ago, here was Harry Lime country, Orson Welles, the Third Man, doing his deadliest deeds from the high-hanging car on the largest ferris wheel in Europe which still functions in the amusement park. His sort of activity has presumably been curtailed of recent years, but who really knows? The opulence of the Hapsburgs, the diplomatic waltzing of the Vienna congress, the political intrigues of post-war Vienna on the road to neutralism – all contribute to the mighty shadows that form the political heritage of this ebullient city. When you look at the buildings of Vienna you see well beyond them into the glittering past.

Where a palace is brilliant and exciting, a Viennese coffee house is almost sacredly understated and peaceful. One Franz George Kolschitzky started the first one, the Blue Bottle, under royal edict back in 1683, but it wasn't until the 18th century that the Viennese coffee house began to assume the political, literary and social importance for which it is so well known today. For a Viennese, his coffee house is his home away from home. For some, it is more than his home. Here you sip delicious coffee, eat fantastic pastries, read newspapers, argue politics (softly), play cards, stare out the window, shoot billiards – and all at your own pace. You stay as long as you like, eat or drink as much or as little as you like, entertain whom you like with whatever degree of patience or energy you feel like expending, and you leave whenever you like without any prior managerial pressure. This luxury of time is unique and precious. You are a patron, a person whose comfort and ease is important and acknowledged. The work-a-day world remains strictly outside as you ruminate in the pleasurable atmosphere of your own quiet, peaceful place. This is the Viennese coffee house.

In the past, some have been the site of great musical events, most especially in June 1814 when the patrons of the Erstes Kaffeehaus listened while Beethoven first played his B flat trio with two of his friends. Arthur Schnitzler used to hold forth in the cafe Griensteidl as did the author of Bambi, (his name was Felix

Salten). Remember, too, this is the city that gave the world Sigmund Freud, indisputably one of the great influences of the century. Here, a coffee house named after Mozart is not an illusionary affectation, but implies some direct and very real relationship with the composer. Also the waltz was born, nurtured and presented to the world, all from the heart of this city.

Palaces stand for the past and here in Vienna, their presence seems uniquely relevant. At the least they are beautiful sights to behold – perhaps their influence on contemporary life is more than can be discerned at first glance. They are certainly opulent mirrors of a day gone by, and even if we are relatively uninvolved, we cannot deny their fascination.

For contemporary Vienna, the coffee house is the most influential, albeit informal, meeting place of all. It offers unique physcological comforts and embodies the special elements of social graces that have become the hallmarks of Vienna. Each, the Palace and the coffee house, in its own way contributes to the structure of this city on the Danube, this charming monument to the past, this pulsating capital of modern-day middle Europe. This Vienna.

Palais Liechtenstein.

View from the arcades of the City Hall towards the neo-gothic "Votio Church".

Everyone is looking at Schönbrunn Palace.

A forbidding door.

Belvedere Palace.

Belvedere Palace.

Schönbrunn Palace.

A less forbidding door   it's open.

17

A good, full view of Schönbrunn Palace.

Palais auf der Wieden — Le Palais.

Fountain outside the side entrance of the Opera House.

View from Hafburg over Heldenplatz to "Heldentor". In front is the equestrian statue of Prince Eugene of Savoy.

Staircase of Palais Kinsky.

Heldenplatz.

This is not a palace – it is
the principal staircase in City Hall.

Josefsplatz in Hafburg.

Heldenplatz, the Place of Heroes, containing the tomb of the Unknown Soldier.

Johann Strauss Memorial in the City Park.

A carriage from the Hapsburg Court – this is in the Wagenburg in Schönbrunn Palace.

The "Schöne Brunnen" — beautiful fountains which gave the name to Schönbrunn Castle. A Hapsburg Prince originally stumbled upon them during a hunting trip.

The Hofburg.

Vienna State Opera Ball — opened by 180 young
couples and the State Opera Ballet.

The flower parterre of Schönbrunn Palace seen from the Neptune fountain.

Inside the Auersperg Palace that belonged to the Rafranos, the family of the Rosenkavalier

The Spanish Riding School.

Snow on Parliament steps. In front, the Statue of Justice.

View from Ringstrasse toward the City Hall.

Night view of the Natural History Museum.

Schönbrunn Palace at night.

Café Landtmann on Kingstrasse.

Karlskirche, St. Charles' Church, by night.

A fiacre on Kohlmart.

A night session at the Spanish Riding School.

The Rathaus, Town Hall.

Café Auersperg in Auersperg Palace.

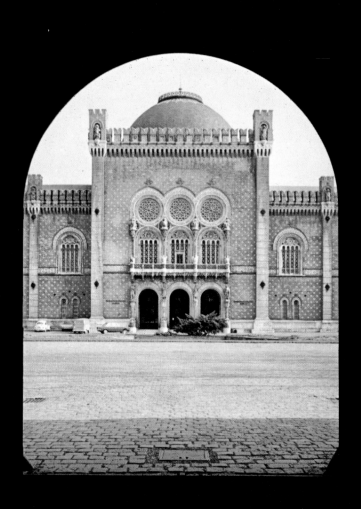

The Opera House.

Café Korb – a traditional coffee shop in the centre
of the city, behind St. Peter's Church.

Café Auersperg.

Café Alte Backstube.

Some Ladies play cards at the Café Eiles . . .

... While others discuss the view from Café Cobenzl.

Café Sperl.

Libresso, a new kind of café in Alte Schmiede.

The State Archives in the Hofberg Palace of the Hapsburgs.

Café Museum. Some coffee drinking, much chess playing.

84

The Vienna Philharmonic Orchestra in concert.

Physical exercise at the Café Sperl.

Sedentary pleasure at the Café Museum.

(Bottom) — Café Museum.

The elegance of the Hotel Sacher
immediately behind the Opera House

Café Landtmann.

Café Hawelka, intellectual meeting place in Dorotheergasse.

Café Hawelka.

Café Kröger.

Café Landtmann.

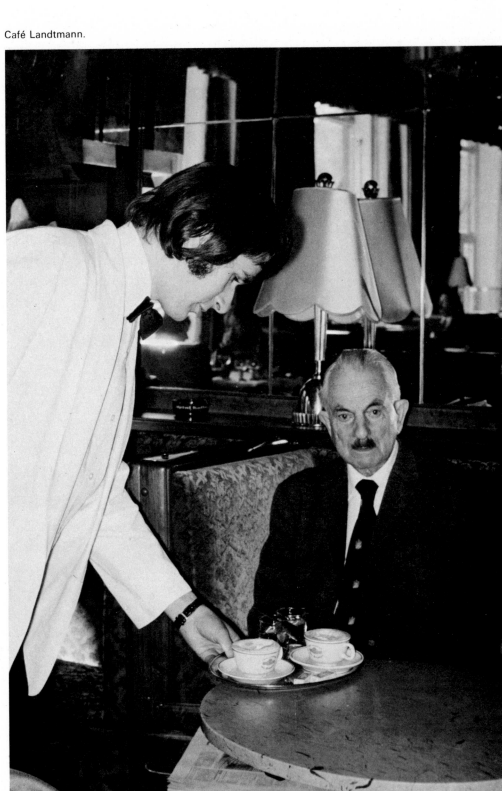

Demel's — Vienna's famous pastry shop.

Café Hawelka.

Café Museum.

Café Sperl.

Some personal politics at the Café Hawelka...

. . . Also at the Café Landtmann.

Café Ritter.

112

Votivkirche – The Votive Church.

Quiet, unhurried service at the Café Museum.

Tired feet at the Café Alte Backstube.

Some casual sunning across the street from the Aurgtheater.

Inside Demel's.

The outdoor garden at the Café Augsperg.

Coffee machine used in 1847 in Café Griensteidl.

Pastry at the Sluka.

Whenever possible Viennese food and drink
is served *mit schlag* (heavy whipped cream).